TIME OUT

A DREAM VISION

ALISHA KUMARI

DEDICATIION

To my parents

Who has always believed in and supported me

Senthil Kumar

&

Issa Chandrashekar

Contents

Part 1

I saw my husband carrying my child in his arms

His face was so pale and dull

Our house was so bright painted in white

The Sparkling white light shone my eyes blind

Unbearable, I covered my eyes using my palm

Lifted my face above and saw no roof on top

I could see the crystal clear sky filled with candy blue snow white clouds

The whole mansion was utter silence

I was panting as my heart pounding

I wandered inside the unaccustomed house searching for the rest of the habitants.

But couldn't find any

The place was desolate in peace and utter silence

I was thrilled and rushed to the balcony

I hardly heard sound on this earth

I was stupefied went rushing and leaned over the bar

I saw a huge cloud floating, holding my house

I couldn't see my feet they were buried into those snowy clouds

The whole place was scattered by snowy clouds

I was baffled for a minute

Immediately I touched my face, body and hair

It was ice cold

I rushed into the house

Turned towards my husband And asked

What happened to me and to our house?

Is this a dream or we are dead of natural calamity along with house
?

He didn't even turn towards me.

Pretended he couldn't hear me.

But my baby turned and smiled at me.

I got more anxious and frightened

And confirmed I'm dead

I went near to my husband and screamed

To my shock

He didn't react

I was totally broken and confused

I yelled in the hall for a minute

Nobody came out hearing me

I sat beside my husband devastated

I followed him as he stood up and went into our room

He stopped in front of the wall

where our portraits were hanging

I was confused what happened to me

That made him so pale dull and soulless

His eye lids were covered with a tiny drop of tear which carried a
lot of grief

I tried hugging him tight and console

But couldn't

I felt hugging a huge water balloon

My mother in law came in anxiously entered the house scolding
me for not having the right change for a vendor

Took the change herself from a masala box from the kitchen

She didn't even notice if I was there standing or listening to her .

And went back as a storm

As my husband standing in the corner with my baby

I was sitting on the sofa devastated

My grandmother came inside sat and on the sofa

She was looking the floor sobbing

She was so lean and bent almost aged eighty

Bones visible covered by wrinkle skin

I stood up in a corner so still and maze

I was all broken, confused, frustrated inside and sobbing heavily

I saw them all my relatives following one by one

As they climbed the stairs across the hallway entering into the
house

I was exhausted and took rest sitting on the steps

Leaning against the wall Seeing the floor

As tears rolling from my eye, followed the cheeks ended dropping
the end of the chin

Sitting still for an hour

As time passed

There were numerous pairs of slippers and shoes

Overflowed the entrance scattered

I couldn't see a speak of the floor

So…. that's it right?

A voice whispered from the back

I was thrilled and so frightened

My heart was pounding harder than before

I was sweating

Didn't have the guts to turn back and look who is it?

"Move over" said the voice

I glided over my seat and moved

It touched my hand

She was my cousin

I hugged her and shot her with lots questions

What's happening here?

What's happening to me?

How can you hear me?

"We are living our last few hours of life" she said

"What"? I got angry and frustrated

No way, I was all good and healthy

I had plans in life

"Well we all have"

I have a family and a kid to grow old with

I want to see my son growing and live with my husband

Above all

I've always wanted to an to be an author

I haven't written any book,

If I die now ?

Nobody will know that I lived in this world.

Only the photos will carry my name date of birth and death as a
memory

I will have grandkids, daughter in law

Whom I can't meet

My son is not even turned one

I have planned to make his birthday a memorable one

"Hey! Stop!..I can understand but this is it" my cousin replied
angrily

We can't decided when and what time we die

There is no time to lament and cry

I didn't had that much plans as you have

But I felt the same way as you did two hours ago

At least you are married and gave birth to a kid

Which you will be remembered through him

I just joined a job

I'm not married yet and 26. As you are

I hugged her

"At least I have a company here", I said

Sorry if I have hurt you in any way

I didn't get the chance to ask the same to others

We stood up and entered into the house

The hall was filled with people like bee comb

There were three dark pit dug in the centre of the hall

Two opened and one closed with pile of sand

Is this supposed to be ours?

"Yes", she replied

"Go peep the last pit your will see your message" she said

My name and time 01:01 was visible

It seems I'll lay here once my time is over

"Don't waste your time" a quote

Probably every wise person would have said in their own mother
tongue

Through literature and art

I should stop lamenting

I've waste my 25 year doing nothing but studying hard, obedient ,
in love, married , working

Being a sister, a daughter, a mother, a friends excreta

Spending money and time on n buying

Have I lived my life for myself?

Seizing the moment and enjoying it to the fullest

I've almost lived it as I wanted it to be

If these are my last few hours let it be

But it's not content and fulfilled yet

Life is to experience all

I have experienced only a half

Isn't it too soon?

I took a walk inside the house solemnly in solitude and grief

I saw my mother sitting beside my sister consoling her

Both were exhausted but weren't crying

They were betrayed by my death as I was

My husband standing in a corner still

Through there were people crowded

It was grave silent

I pepped onto the pit again terrifically

Gasped and stepped two step back, heart pounding

I turned towards the portrait on the wall.

They were turned towards the wall

I flipped the side

It was a picture of me smiling happy beside husband

a selfie taken five years

I flipped the next portrait

It was gifted by my friend a mosaic portrait of hundred photos of
me and my husband

Memories as young lovers ten years back

Next is our wedding photo all happy and satisfied with dreams of
future

Shining in our eyes

The next of my mom and sister beside me, we were always the
happy three

The next photo took my heart away, it's the picture of my son so
little tiny face

Who believed in me and born

He is still a baby of nine months

Only three Months away for his birthday celebration his big day

But without me

I'll miss him going to school and college

His first word

I still don't know his favorite color or food

We haven't spoken by words but through heart

Will he be longing for me

To greed seeing the love a mother of his friend

He might forget me and my face?

Or looking these portrait in soliloquy

As I'm now

Death is painful, isn't it?

Not to experience of the ache or eternal absence but to make our loved ones cry

Leave them all of a sudden without an adieu

"Oh, god ,

You could have taken my soul without a notice

This is so much painful than dying

You have given me these last few hours

To lamenting blabbering about past and future

To see these beautiful faces turning stale"

I touched the stand filled with all presents, medals and books

I bought recently

Few to be finished and Yet to be read,

These books will stay forever unfinished

The war between immortal and mortal are unresolved issue

Objects and arts stay eternal and immortal

My attire , cosmetics will be until they expires

Now I only stay in the memories of the people who know me,..

And the portrait on the wall

Until those who love my will die

Remembered for a month or 2

I should have taken good care of people who really cared for me

Now People will talk about my character and achievemen

How funny I was and how I treated them

I should have maintain some real friends

All those grief and love

Will fade away as time passes

Once in a year I will be remembered people will cry and lament

But for an year or two

My mother, grandparents, parents or to say accurately

All living beings on this earth

Will be waiting for the day as end and call it as death

My son will be leading his life with his family and kids

But introducing me in a portrait on the wall

Saying "this is my mother, people say she loved me so much"

Few years later one day he might hate me for not being with him

Seeing his friends and Scolding me for not consoling him

As others mother doing

My husband might get married to someone or fall in love again
with someone

For the sake of my son or his carnal pleasure

Or to spend his remaining days with the next partner till his time
expired like mine

All my cousin siblings' parents and relations

Will move on with joy looking forward for the next day and live
their lives

The clock stroke 12 sharp

And All I was left with is an hour time

Time decides everything,

Time is nothing but earth and people in it as a puppet

Time is a power which showers

Luck, wealth, health and also countermand

My small business will stop

My work will be replaced by someone else

My husband will replace me

Two love cant be changed

The one I was born out of and the one I gave birth to

I thank god for giving me extra time to be a mother

For showing me the miracle of life and now death

My things will be abandoned

My body will be demolished with soil or fire

I'll be placed in the dark hollow pit of six feet

A place where people will be remembered of good things

A small tomb built with good words carved with my smiling
photo

Alisha 1996-2022

Remembered for "love & kindness"

Greeting people who will be visiting me in future

The clock stroke 12:45

My cousin went and laid in her space

She didn't lament as much as I did

She didn't say neither thank you nor good bye

She didn't even look me back

I cried for her and for me of no tears

I saw the future which is going to happen within few minutes

At 01:01 I'm the next to be laid

I pepped over the previous coffin saw my aunt lying dead

I wondered why she was dead too?

I guess her time was over before my cousin

I requested for her soul to rest in peace

After all she went through in her life

as a young hard working girl at the age of 12

Married to a drunken psycho

Gave birth to a girl and a boy

Lived her life working

Taking care of her children, parents and her relatives with all
supply

I guess she might not have heard different dishes or travelled much

Or enjoyed hanging out to different places

I pity for the life she has lived

Compared to her, I regret nothing

But procrastinating things

Anger, fight and sometimes stopped talking to people I love

I've spent almost a most a year of not talking to people of anger
and grudge

I've wasted not all but pretty much of my time.

Which now I realize it's worth

Time stops for none, realized too late

I don't have time now

I badly regret for not being what I wanted to be

A writer, author and off course a good mom

I'm definitely going to miss these two

The clock struck to 1:00 all I left with was with one minute

My mother and sister were always been close to my heart

My heart carried so much grief it was so heavy

I wanted to live longer I was in need of more time

I'm going to miss watching those all

I gave goodbye kiss to my baby as he laughed

I guess that He could see me but couldn't understand

Yet he is just a baby

Will he at least convey this to other or even remember

Will people remember me?

For what I have done

Every last rituals will be decided by the people

The place, flower, color, time etc

I can't give my suggestion or opinion

I'm not allowed to take any of the memories

All I have is to rest in peace in dark, solitude and silence

With no past or morrow

With no task no ornament, money, fame, passion.

My love was immense

I hope he will take my loss gracefully as I did

I've lost all grief, anger, grudge that bothered me

Death is the end of time

That I understand only the seconds of it

I could feel the seconds of my life

I wasn't allowed to say goodbye or explain or exchange few words

All of a sudden my life changed

I'm all alone now living last seconds between death and time

The battle is really hard

It's not about life and death its always about the time

Random of thoughts I remember the lines once said by wilde

"Death must be so beautiful to lie in the soft brown earth with grass waving above ones head and listen to the silence"

To have no yesterday no tomorrow

To forget time, to forget life to be at peace "

I see people filling the hall placing the tomb centre watching the death as an adventure to be

experienced soon that is negotiable adventure

Waiting to experience next.

I'll remain only in the memory of a very few people

And that art I've bonded

once born once died

I was Paralyzing in fear

A fear of time running out

I didn't want to be an immortal but to leave behind a deed that
will carry my name

For centuries like Shakespeare or Jackson

I'll be able to see my ancestors and thank them for their talents
and beauty passed over me

I've kept myself busy

The power of the death full on rage has put an end to my toil

No more pain , yelling nor sweat

In flash of second

Endless sleep , dream forever

I wanted to be an flash of second

Without knowing a dream that will contain a sleeping forever

I couldn't ask for wishes but more time to say au revoir , a adieu
kiss

I was floating carried by the air

Last five seconds left

I was crying my droplets from eyes were floating as scattered pearls

I felt no gravity

No life no death …….

Beautifully

Laid down in the coffin

My heart was still pounding

I kept my hand on my chest praising my heart "You've done a great job".

Thank you!

Now you can rest… in peace

I rubbed my hands all over my body

Thanking them all I loved myself always

Tomorrow will be great for people without me.

I wont be there to see any

Sleep my body soul and …

I touched all over my body feeling my skin

Appreciating them, I loved myself always

Wishing Tomorrow will be great for people.

I won't be there to see any

Sleep my body soul and mind

Tears of those loved me over graves

The pain of words left unsaid and deeds left undone

This death is going to be an big adventure

I'm ready

A part of me is inherited in my child

I hope he will be a great artist like me

Or make people remember me with his actions, manner, and talent

I'll be waiting to met you

Somewhere someday

Time out

The was a last stroke call bell

As I closed my eyes

Everything stopped became dark and chill

A shinny light like candle flaming high

It vacuumed me

I followed it

I wasn't breathing or feel my heart pounding

It was cold and no gravity

Dark and a quiet place

I heard a Sound that raised from fade

Heard a baby wailing

I ignored the light followed the sound

Heavy Gasp as I was smothered

I woke up all of a sudden

Sleeping in my warm cozy bed

Beside my husband and baby

My husband patted my back "Nightmare?"

I'm alive thank god

Is this a vision or message of life and time

To preach the mortals,

about TIME.

www.ingramcontent.com/pod-product-compliance
Lightning Source LLC
Chambersburg PA
CBHW070731160726
48003CB00006BA/2446